POP ROCK

Popular Rock Superstars of Yesterday and Today

AC/DC

Aerosmith

The Allman
Brothers Band

The Beatles

Billy Joel

Bob Marley
and the Wailers

Bruce Springsteen

The Doors

Elton John

The Grateful Dead

Led Zeppelin

Lynyrd Skynyrd

Pink Floyd

Queen

The Rolling
Stones

U2

The Who

Elton John

Ethan Schlesinger

Mason Crest Publishers

Elton John

FRONTIS From Rocket Man to Sir, Elton John has had a long and prestigious career in music.

Produced by 21st Century Publishing and Communications, Inc.

Editorial by Harding House Publishing Services, Inc.

MASON CREST PUBLISHERS INC.
370 Reed Road
Broomall, Pennsylvania 19008
(866) MCP-BOOK (toll free)
www.masoncrest.com

Printed in the United States.

First Printing

9 8 7 6 5 4 3 2 1

Library of Congress Cataloging-in-Publication Data

Schlesinger, Ethan.
  Elton John / Ethan Schlesinger.
    p. cm. — (Popular rock superstars of yesterday and today)
  Includes bibliographical references (p.   ) and index.
  Hardback edition: ISBN-13: 978-1-4222-0189-3
  Paperback edition: ISBN-13: 978-1-4222-0316-3
 1. John, Elton—Juvenile literature. 2. Rock musicians—England—Biography—
Juvenile literature. I. Title.
ML3930.J58S35 2008
782.42166092—dc22
[B]   2007021461

CONTENTS

ROCK 'N' ROLL TIMELINE

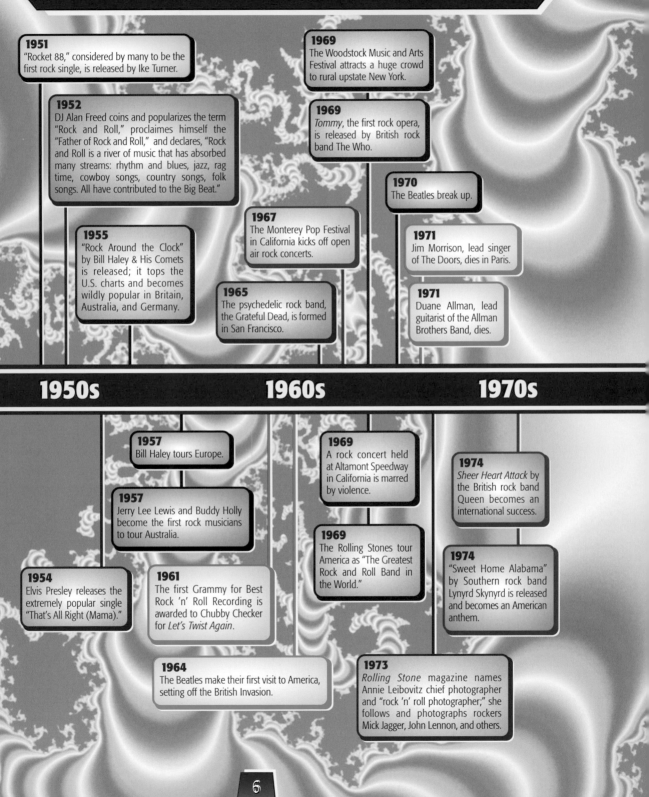

1951
"Rocket 88," considered by many to be the first rock single, is released by Ike Turner.

1952
DJ Alan Freed coins and popularizes the term "Rock and Roll," proclaimes himself the "Father of Rock and Roll," and declares, "Rock and Roll is a river of music that has absorbed many streams: rhythm and blues, jazz, rag time, cowboy songs, country songs, folk songs. All have contributed to the Big Beat."

1955
"Rock Around the Clock" by Bill Haley & His Comets is released; it tops the U.S. charts and becomes wildly popular in Britain, Australia, and Germany.

1967
The Monterey Pop Festival in California kicks off open air rock concerts.

1965
The psychedelic rock band, the Grateful Dead, is formed in San Francisco.

1969
The Woodstock Music and Arts Festival attracts a huge crowd to rural upstate New York.

1969
Tommy, the first rock opera, is released by British rock band The Who.

1970
The Beatles break up.

1971
Jim Morrison, lead singer of The Doors, dies in Paris.

1971
Duane Allman, lead guitarist of the Allman Brothers Band, dies.

1950s   1960s   1970s

1957
Bill Haley tours Europe.

1957
Jerry Lee Lewis and Buddy Holly become the first rock musicians to tour Australia.

1954
Elvis Presley releases the extremely popular single "That's All Right (Mama)."

1961
The first Grammy for Best Rock 'n' Roll Recording is awarded to Chubby Checker for *Let's Twist Again*.

1964
The Beatles make their first visit to America, setting off the British Invasion.

1969
A rock concert held at Altamont Speedway in California is marred by violence.

1969
The Rolling Stones tour America as "The Greatest Rock and Roll Band in the World."

1973
Rolling Stone magazine names Annie Leibovitz chief photographer and "rock 'n' roll photographer;" she follows and photographs rockers Mick Jagger, John Lennon, and others.

1974
Sheer Heart Attack by the British rock band Queen becomes an international success.

1974
"Sweet Home Alabama" by Southern rock band Lynyrd Skynyrd is released and becomes an American anthem.

1987
Billy Joel becomes the first American rock star to perform in the Soviet Union since the construction of the Berlin Wall.

2005
Led Zeppelin is ranked #1 on VH1's list of the 100 Greatest Artists of Hard Rock.

1985
Rock stars perform at Live Aid, a benefit concert to raise money to fight Ethiopian famine.

2005
Many rock groups participate in Live 8, a series of concerts to raise awareness of extreme poverty in Africa.

2003
Led Zeppelin's "Stairway to Heaven" is inducted into the Grammy Hall of Fame.

1980
John Lennon of the Beatles is murdered in New York City.

2000s
Aerosmith's album sales reach 140 million worldwide and the group becomes the bestselling American hard rock band of all time.

1975
Tommy, the movie, is released.

2007
Billy Joel become the first person to sing the National Anthem before two Super Bowls.

1975
Time magazine features Bruce Springsteen on its cover as "Rock's New Sensation."

1995
The Rock and Roll Hall of Fame and Museum opens in Cleveland, Ohio.

1970s   1980s   1990s   2000s

1979
Pink Floyd's *The Wall* is released.

1991
Freddie Mercury, lead vocalist of the British rock group Queen, dies of AIDS.

2004
Elton John receives a Kennedy Center Honor.

1979
The first Grammy for Best Rock Vocal Performance by a Duo or Group is awarded to The Eagles.

2004
Rolling Stone Magazine ranks The Beatles #1 of the 100 Greatest Artists of All Time, and Bob Dylan #2.

1986
The Rolling Stones receive a Grammy Lifetime Achievement Award.

1981
MTV goes on the air.

2006
U2 wins five more Grammys, for a total of 22—the most of any rock artist or group.

1986
The first Rock and Roll Hall of Fame induction ceremony is held; Chuck Berry, Little Richard, Ray Charles, Elvis Presley, and James Brown, are among the first inductees.

1981
For Those About to Rock We Salute You by Australian rock band AC/DC becomes the first hard rock album to reach #1 in the U.S.

2006
Bob Dylan, at age 65, releases *Modern Times* which immediately rises to #1 in the U.S.

The world mourned when England's Princess Diana was killed in an auto accident in Paris. At the funeral, Elton performed a new version of his famous "Candle in the Wind," which had been written about Marilyn Monroe. The 1997 version written by Elton and his long-time writing partner Bernie Taupin refers to the princess as "England's rose."

Saying Goodbye

The year 1997 was a hard one for rock star Elton John. When John Lennon was shot in 1980, Elton had learned the pain of losing a good friend to a tragic and violent act. But now, he had to relearn that same agonizing lesson, not once but twice in the same year.

A Friend's Funeral

Designer Gianni Versace was known both for his outrageous fashions for women—and for his loyalty as a friend. A *National Review* article published after his death described Versace as:

> **"a cultivated, brilliant man, by all accounts loyal, decent, and blessed with a talent for friendship. He was a generous, hard-working, . . . solid citizen who demonstrated that a family business can thrive in a global economy."**

When Versace was gunned down on the steps of his own home, the world was horrified.

Versace's death was particularly hard for Elton John, who had been his friend for years. The two men had a lot in common: both were homosexuals, both loved to have fun in extravagant ways, both were generous friends. In a 2002 interview, Elton told Larry King:

> **"He was like a brother, really. We were both very much the same. We were both very impulsive. We both loved life. We both loved shopping. We both had a love of clothes, obviously, because he was the designer that I kind of wore forever and ever. I mean, I haven't really switched allegiances since. Even since his death I've, you know, I still wear Versace a lot. . . . He was just the brother I never had. And we had such a great time together."**

At Versace's funeral, Elton turned to another good friend for comfort: Britain's Princess Diana. A famous photograph catches the two in what looks as though is a moment of shared grief. In the same Larry King interview, Elton explained what really happened:

> **"I was a mess. Johnny was my best, one of my best friends. I loved him dearly, as did Diana. And there was a very famous scene. . . . Actually, she wasn't really propping me up. I had a roll of mints, and I was asking her if she'd like a mint. And she said yes. So we've both got our head bowed. But I was, I was very upset. I was crying, and she was incredibly supportive, and incredibly—those years of being stoic and being kind of cool in the . . . in the public eye served her very well at that occasion. It didn't serve me very well because I was a complete mess."**

The Second Tragedy

Just a few months later, Princess Diana, the one who had comforted Elton at his friend's funeral, was also dead. This time, Elton would be called on to sing at the funeral.

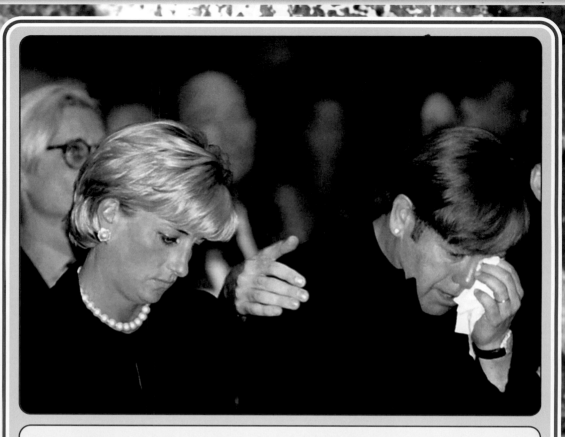

Just a few months before Princess Diana's death, she and Elton attended the funeral of their mutual friend Gianni Versace. The famous Italian fashion designer had been murdered outside his Miami, Florida, home by spree killer Andrew Cunanan. Elton called Gianni one of his best friends, and his murder saddened him deeply.

But what would he sing? Dazed with his own grief, he knew he couldn't write something fast enough that would be good enough to honor his friend. And yet he was honored to be asked, and he wanted to use his music to help the world mourn the woman so many had loved so much.

Earlier, Elton had released a song called "Candle in the Wind" as a tribute to Marilyn Monroe (whose real name was Norma Jean). Now, Elton and his lyricist, Bernie Taupin, decided to create a new version of the song, one with words referring specifically to Diana:

" Goodbye, England's rose,
May you ever grow in our hearts.
You were the grace that placed itself
Where lives were torn apart.
You called out to our country
And you whispered to those in pain.
Now you belong to heaven
And the stars spell out your name. "

Princess Diana's funeral on September 6, 1997, was for invited guests only. Millions more all over the world watched the service on television. Among them were more than a million mourners in London's Hyde Park. After Elton played "Candle in the Wind," the Hyde Park crowd gave the singer a standing ovation.

Elton sang the new song at Diana's funeral at Westminster Abbey. Later, he told Larry King:

“As a commercial, pop singer to be asked to do this was kind of revolutionary. And so when I did the rehearsal the day before, I insisted on a teleprompter, because I thought, if I sing this, and I sing 'Goodbye Norma Jean,' because I didn't know what kind of state I was going to be in on the day of the actual funeral. I just thought, I've got to get this right. And it was an amazing thing. I mean, it was—I had to call on all my kind of years of professionalism, and all my experience, because I didn't want to break down and become emotional. I thought that was—I was doing the job of making everybody else feel emotional. And if I started to be emotional, I thought that would make it—it would **denigrate** the occasion, and it would make it more morguish than it maybe already was, you know.”

After Diana's funeral, the recording "Candle in the Wind 1997" became the fastest-selling single of all time. More than 30 million copies were sold worldwide, and approximately £55 million in proceeds were donated to the Diana, Princess of Wales Memorial Fund. Later, the song won Elton the Grammy for the Best Male Pop Vocal Performance.

But Elton never sang the song again. In his long and **prolific** career, he had written literally hundreds of songs and made millions of dollars. But this song was special. It belonged to his friend, Princess Diana, a kind and gracious woman who had died too young.

And yet her song would become part of the legend that is Elton John, a legend with many chapters that began more than sixty years ago.

Even while still wearing short pants, Elton—then Reginald Dwight—showed that he had what it took to be a musician. Music filled the household, and young Reginald drank it all in. His proud parents often asked him to entertain at their parties, and he loved all the attention.

The Early Days of a Legend

In 1947, in the outskirts of London, a son was born to Stanley Dwight and his wife Sheila. They named him Reginald Kenneth, never dreaming that when their son grew up, he would take a new name for himself. The world would never recognize the name Reginald Dwight—but everyone would know Elton John!

Elton's Childhood

Stanley Dwight was a Royal Air Force officer who was frequently away from home. When he *was* there, he was a stern and demanding father—but he also took time to share his love of music with his son. Stanley had been a trumpet player with a **big band** called Bob Miller and the Milkmen, and he and his wife filled their home with music, playing the records of great pianists like Winifred Atwell and Nat King Cole, as well as the music of singers like Frank Sinatra and Rosemary Clooney. This was the music

Reginald grew up hearing, soaking the melodies and rhythms into his mind and soul.

When their son was only three years old, Stanley and Sheila began giving him piano lessons. By the time he was four, they knew he was talented. Proud of their son's musical accomplishments, they often asked him to play at parties.

In grade school, Reginald continued to develop his musical skill. He won a scholarship to the Royal Academy of Music when he was eleven, where his teachers were impressed with his talent. His peers probably resented him sometimes: Reginald dashed off last-minute melodies for his composition assignments that ended up being better than anyone else's in the class.

Young Reginald, however, liked playing by ear better than using sheet music, whether it was his own original composition or a famous composer's. One of his teachers from the academy remembered that when Reginald first entered her class, she played a four-page piece by Handel—which Reginald proceeded to play back as though he were a "gramophone record."

Reginald enjoyed playing classical composers like Chopin and Bach, and he liked singing in the choir as well. As an adult, however, Elton said:

"I kind of resented going to the Academy. I was one of those children who could just about get away without practicing and still pass, scrape through the grades."

Truth was, Reginald liked rock 'n' roll better than he liked classical music. His mother's tastes leaned toward Elvis Presley, and Reginald's own collection of rock records was growing. His father did not approve; he wanted Reginald to concentrate on the classics. Meanwhile, although Reginald's mother liked rock 'n' roll, too, her son's fascination with Little Richard frightened her. When Reginald started singing and playing like Jerry Lee Lewis at his grammar school, the adults in his life did not approve!

When Reginald was fifteen, his parents' marriage ended. His mother remarried, and Reginald's new stepfather, Fred Farebrother (whom Reginald called "Derf"), encouraged his stepson to begin his music career.

Training in classical music could not dampen Reginald's fascination with rock music. Jerry Lee Lewis and Little Richard were major influences on the budding star's music, much to the dismay of his parents and other adults in his life. His first long-term gig was at a pub, where he played rock, country, and Irish songs to its sometimes-drunken patrons.

Elton's Early Career

Reginald's first long-term gig was at the Northwood Hills Pub, where for several years he played the piano on the weekends. "During that whole period, I don't think I ever missed a gig," Elton said later. The pub's patrons were a rough crowd, and occasionally, someone who had had too much to drink would dump a beer into Reginald's piano. Reginald learned to smile and keep playing, everything from country songs to Irish folk tunes to the day's current hits. He even threw in a few songs he'd written himself.

When Reginald was seventeen, he and his friends got together a band they called Bluesology. Done with school, Reginald made a living of sorts by running errands during the day for a music publishing company and dividing his nights between solo gigs and performances with Bluesology. By 1965, the band was doing backup for the British tours of American **soul** and **R&B** musicians such as the Isley Brothers and Patti LaBelle and the Bluebelles. The following year, the group became musician Long John Baldry's supporting band on his tours of English cabarets.

A Partnership Is Born

Meanwhile, Reginald answered an advertisement placed by Liberty Records. At the interview, Liberty's manager gave him a stack of lyrics written by Bernie Taupin, who had answered the same ad. Reginald wrote music for the lyrics and mailed them off to Bernie. Although the two did not meet for another eighteen months, a lifelong partnership was born. Their first song, "Scarecrow," was recorded in 1967.

Meet Elton John

By the time Bernie and Reginald met in person, Reginald was no longer Reginald. In honor of Long John Baldry and Bluesology's saxophonist Elton Dean, the young musician had decided to legally change his name to Elton John.

In 1968, Elton and Bernie teamed up as staff songwriters for DJM Records. Over the next two years, they wrote easy-listening material for many different artists. Bernie usually took less than an hour to write the lyrics, then he'd pass them along to Elton. If Elton couldn't write music for the lyrics in less than half an hour, he threw the lyrics in the wastebasket.

In 1967, the first of many songs written by Elton and Bernie Taupin was released. Few songwriting teams have had the long-term success as this dynamic duo. Bernie's lyrics and Elton's music are a winning combination. The pair got their start writing songs for other performers, but soon Elton began recording them.

During this time, Elton also played the piano for the Hollies when they recorded "He Ain't Heavy, He's My Brother," and he sang backup vocals for the Scaffold, a rock trio that included Beatle Paul McCartney's brother. Finally, Elton began doing his own recording with DJM of more complex songs he and Bernie created. The first were singles, "I've Been Loving You" and "Lady Samantha," followed by an entire album, *Empty Sky*. Elton's records were reviewed well—but they didn't sell.

Elton's *real* career still hadn't begun.

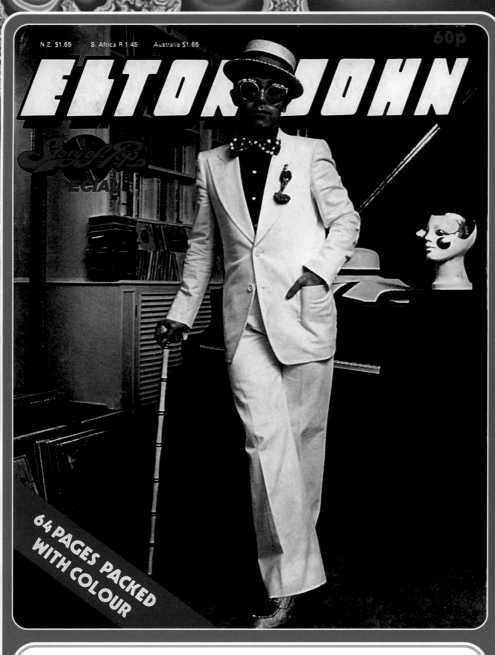

ELTON JOHN

Story of Pop SPECIAL

64 PAGES PACKED WITH COLOUR

As the decade of the seventies dawned, so did a new rock star—Elton John, Rocket Man. Sometimes clad in outrageous costumes and sometimes more traditionally, like here on the cover of *Elton John—Story of Pop*, fans were never quite sure what to expect from Elton—except great music.

Rocket Man

Despite the poor sales of Elton's first records, he and Bernie weren't about to give up. In 1970, DJM Records put out a new album, *Elton John* (released in the United States by Uni Records). The album contained rock ballads that sounded a little like **gospel** and played on people's emotions.

Elton Finds Fame

The album's first single, "Border Song," barely made it to the U.S. top-100; it peaked at #92. The second single, however, "Your Song," made the top-10, and so did the album. On the heels of this success, Elton's first American concert was booked at the Troubadour in Los Angeles.

Elton cast aside his inhibitions at the concert. He went back to his old days in grammar school when he hammed it up like Jerry Lee Lewis: he kicked over the piano bench and did handstands on the keyboard. The critics were impressed with his talent, though, and musicians Quincy Jones and Bob Dylan were as well.

Album After Album

Elton's next album, *Tumbleweed Connection*, came out that same year in October. It shot up *Billboard*'s top-10 almost immediately. The following month, Elton recorded a live album, *11-17-70* (or *17-11-70* in Britain), which showcased his talent as something new on the rock scene—a rock pianist. The album was taped at a live show aired from WABC-FM in New York City. It included many of Elton and Bernie's early compositions, demonstrating the gospel and **boogie-woogie** influences on their music.

Years later, Billy Joel, another rock pianist, wrote of Elton John in *Rolling Stone* magazine:

> **"Before him, rock was . . . guitar-based singer-songwriter stuff. Elton brought back fantastic piano-based rock. Elton knows what his instrument is capable of. The piano is a percussion instrument, like a drum. . . . Elton . . . always had that rhythmic, very African, syncopated style that comes from being well versed in gospel and good old R&B."**

Elton and Bernie followed up the live album with the soundtrack for the movie *Friends*, and then yet another album, *Madman Across the Water*. The song "Friends" from the soundtrack became a hit, and so did "Levon" from *Madman*. The album itself reached *Billboard*'s top-10.

The Elton John Band

By 1972, Elton had gathered his band: Davey Johnstone provided the guitar and backing vocals; Nigel Olsson was on drums; and Dee Murray played bass. The next five albums were the result of the magic created by the band members' talents combined with Elton and Bernie's writing skills, producer Gus Dudgeon's guidance, and Elton's **flamboyant** performances.

The band released *Honky Château*, Elton's first #1 album in the United States; it spent five weeks at the top of the charts. Two hit

singles came from it as well: "Rocket Man (I Think It's Going to Be a Long, Long Time)" and "Honky Cat."

At the beginning of 1973, the band put out yet another album, this time with MCA Records: *Don't Shoot Me, I'm Only the Piano Player*, which spawned another two hits, "Crocodile Rock" and "Daniel." "Crocodile Rock" was Elton's first single to make it to #1 in the United States. (Meanwhile, though, Elton's singles weren't as popular back home in the United Kingdom.)

In the early 1970s, Elton settled on the musicians that would form his band. Rounding out his sound were (from top right) Davey Johnstone (on guitar and backup vocals), Nigel Olsson (on drums), Ray Cooper (playing percussion), and Dee Murray (on bass guitar). The dapper guy between Dee and Davey is Elton, of course.

That same year, the band released what many still consider to be Elton's best album, *Goodbye Yellow Brick Road*, a double album that was loved by the critics while it topped the charts both in the United States and the UK. The singles "Bennie and the Jets," "Goodbye Yellow Brick Road," "Candle in the Wind," and "Saturday Night's Alright for Fighting" all came from the album.

Elton's Other Work

With success after success under his belt, Elton decided to form his own label, Rocket Records (distributed by MCA), and signed on artists in whom he took a personal interest, including Neil Sedaka and Kiki Dee. Instead of releasing his own records through Rocket, however, Elton opted for an $8 million contract with MCA. (Once the contract was signed, MCA is rumored to have taken out a $25 million insurance policy on Elton's life.)

In 1974, Elton collaborated with John Lennon; Elton **covered** the Beatles' "Lucy in the Sky with Diamonds" and Lennon's "One Day at a Time," while the Elton John Band was featured on Lennon's "Whatever Gets You Through the Night." The pair performed both hits at Madison Square Garden in what would be John Lennon's last live performance. By this point in his career, Lennon hated stage appearances—but he had promised Elton that he would join him on stage if "Whatever Gets You Through the Night" became a #1 hit.

And *More* Albums

You might think Elton would have been so busy he wouldn't have had time to create more albums—but in 1974, *Caribou* was released and made it to #1. Recorded quickly between live appearances (rumor has it that the band only spent two weeks on the album), critics weren't impressed with the album's quality. Despite this, two songs from the album—"The Bitch Is Back" and "Don't Let the Sun Go Down on Me"—were both hit singles. At the end of 1974, yet another album, *Elton John's Greatest Hits*, came out and reached #1 on the *Billboard* list.

The new album in 1975, *Captain Fantastic and the Brown Dirt Cowboy*, was far more autobiographical than anything Elton and Bernie had written before. Bernie's lyrics described their past as struggling songwriters, and the hit single "Someone Saved My Life Tonight" referred to an actual incident in Elton's life.

Elton joined another rock legend in 1974 when he collaborated with former Beatle John Lennon. Elton released covers of "Lucy in the Sky with Diamonds" and "One Day at a Time." His band performed with John Lennon on "Whatever Gets You Through the Night." Elton and John performed together at John's last live performance.

Tommy

A very different sort of opportunity came along for Elton that same year: Pete Townshend of The Who asked him to play the role of the Pinball Wizard in his rock opera *Tommy*. Elton also performed the song by the same name. His version was used in the movie and the single also came out that year.

Major Changes

After so much creative activity, it's no wonder that Elton was stressed, tired, and grumpy. He fired two members of his band, Olsson and Murray, although they were responsible in large part for the unique sound of his live performances. Kenny Passarelli took over the bass,

Elton John the Pinball Wizard? Well, that's what Pete Townshend of The Who thought when he asked Elton to play the role in his rock opera *Tommy***. Looking back, the casting might not have been as far-fetched as one might think. Elton also performed the song in the movie and released it as a single.**

and Roger Pope picked up the drums. The new rhythm section created a heavier backbeat for Elton's voice. James Newton-Howard also joined up to do studio arrangements and play the keyboards.

The first album by the new band, *Rock of the Westies*, entered the U.S. charts at #1, but the critics did not like the sound produced by this new version of the Elton John Band. Despite this, Elton was raking in the money, mostly from his concerts.

Elton the Rock Idol?

You might think Elton John was an unlikely person to be a rock star. After all, he was short, chubby, balding, and wore glasses. But he had developed an outrageous fashion sense that helped give him a unique stage presence. His wardrobe included ostrich feathers and flashing-light glasses, and he was famous for dressing up as characters, from Donald Duck to Wolfgang Amadeus Mozart. During his performances, his behavior was as over the top as his clothes. Concertgoers loved him.

Journalist Mike Quigley described Elton's appearance when he interviewed him early in the 1970s:

> **"Elton John . . . sporting a short-cropped Julius Caesar shag haircut, . . . sunglasses, yellow and green velveteen trousers, a white ruffled Liberace shirt with a blue serge-ish midicoat, white patent leather boots, and a large Donald Duck button on his right lapel."**

Typical Elton attire! According to Billy Joel,

> **"Inside Elton's dressing room there are a thousand pairs of sunglasses, a hundred pairs of shoes and about fifty Versace suits laid out."**

In the spring of 1976, the unlikely rock star produced yet another live album, *Here and There*, followed by *Blue Moves* the following fall, which contained the single "Sorry Seems to Be the Hardest Word." That year his single "Don't Go Breaking My Heart" topped both the U.S. and UK charts.

Slowing Down

Elton had been creating albums at the same frantic, passionate pace that characterized his live performances. In 1977, he decided to take a break, and he announced he was retiring from the concert scene. Bernie began collaborating with other musicians, and Elton hid himself away in one or another of his three mansions; he only came out to attend football (what Americans calls soccer) matches where his favorite team, Watford, played. (Later, he bought the team.)

Elton hadn't stopped creating, but now, he only put out one album a year. *A Single Man* came out in 1978, written with lyricist Gary Osborne, but the album produced no top-20 singles. The following year, Elton was once more on the charts with "Mama Can't Buy You Love," but the disco-influenced album *Victim of Love* was not received well by either the critics or his fans.

Although Elton worked with other lyricists during this period, he and Bernie reunited for the 1980 album, *21 at 33*. The single from this album, "Little Jeannie" (with lyrics by Gary Osborne) reached #3 on the U.S. charts. In 1981, *The Fox* included Elton's collaborations with several lyricists.

Death of a Friend

In September of 1980, Elton performed at a free concert for 400,000 fans in New York City's Central Park, within earshot of John Lennon's apartment building. Three months later, John Lennon was shot and killed in front of the same building. In Elton's 1982 album, *Jump Up!*, he mourned the loss of his friend with the song "Empty Garden (Hey Hey Johnny)." When he performed the tribute song at a sold-out Madison Square Garden show, John Lennon's widow, Yoko Ono, and his son, Sean Ono Lennon (Elton's godchild), joined him on stage.

Personal Upheavals

The 1980s were not an easy decade for Elton. In 1984, he surprised the world by marrying sound engineer Renate Blauel; most people had always assumed Elton was gay. The marriage only lasted four years, and Elton eventually confirmed that yes, he was a homosexual. Then in 1986, Elton lost his voice while on tour in Australia. Later, Elton admitted his heavy marijuana use had contributed to his condition. He needed surgery, and his voice would never hit the high notes where it once soared.

What's short, chubby, balding, bespectacled, and arrayed in over-the-top costumes? Why a rock legend of course! Elton John, that is. Feathers, furs, and flashing glasses soon became as much a part of an Elton John performance as the man and his music. Elton may have had fun with his costumes—but he was serious about his music.

His songs were hits through the '80s, but they didn't climb as high on the charts as they had in the 1970s. Nevertheless, "I'm Still Standing" and "I Guess That's Why They Call It the Blues" both made it to the top-10 lists. Elton kept on recording, but the years were taking their toll. Marijuana wasn't the only drug he abused; he had a long habit of handling his life's stresses with cocaine and alcohol. Years afterward, he said:

I'm still standing.

Want strong bones?
Drinking enough
lowfat milk
now can help prevent
osteoporosis later.

got milk?

Got milk? By the end of the 1980s, Elton was so popular he was one of the many stars of stage, screen, television, sports, and music to appear in "Got Milk?" advertisements. Despite his popularity, Elton had been through a lot in the 1980s, and few people were probably happier than he was to see the decade end.

"Sometimes when I'm flying over the Alps I think, 'That's all the cocaine I sniffed.' We once tried to figure out how much money we spent on coke and alcohol. We were so disgusted that we stopped.**"**

Elton's Helping Hand

Despite his personal troubles, Elton always liked helping others. He was one of the many performers who took part in Live Aid, a concert event held around the world to raise money to aid Africa's famine victims. During the concert, Elton introduced George Michael to viewers, performing "Don't Let the Sun Go Down on Me" with the younger musician.

Elton did all he could to support young artists. He asked George to sing backup vocals for his single "Wrap Her Up," and he recruited Nik Kershaw to do instrumentals on "Nikita." He also recorded material with Millie Jackson. By lending his name and reputation to these younger musicians' performances, Elton gave their careers significant boosts. As Elton said:

"The whole point of being in this business and being blessed and being successful is that you're able to do things for your friends . . . which means that they can have something special in their lives, too.**"**

The End of an Era

In 1988, Elton performed five sold-out shows at New York's Madison Square Garden, giving him a total of twenty-six sold-out shows at this prestigious **venue**. This seemed like a high-water mark for Elton. He decided the time had come to say good-bye to the theatrical personality he had cultivated on stage. At an auction in London, he sold two thousand pieces of **memorabilia** from his career, netting over $20 million. It was almost as though Elton had died.

He was fat, run-down from drug abuse, and exhausted. The Rocket Man had shot so high he was burning.

But Elton didn't die. Instead, he was reborn.

The one thing about success is that it can let you buy lots of toys—including very expensive ones. Elton had been very successful, and he had a lot of very expensive toys, including cars. But that wasn't all. Elton amassed an impressive art collection and owned an English football team.

Elton's Rebirth

"You know," Elton John told Larry King in 2002, "those three words—I need help. If only I'd said them earlier." It wasn't easy for Elton to admit he was in trouble. After all, he seemed to have everything—talent, fame, wealth—and he was embarrassed to admit the truth. Once he did, though, his new life began.

Ryan White's Influence

A teenager was the one who finally gave Elton the courage to face up to his life—but Ryan White's life challenged many people, not just Elton John.

When Ryan was thirteen, he was diagnosed with AIDS. Faced with the question of how he would spend his remaining time, all Ryan wanted was a normal life. This was 1984, however, and many people were still ignorant about AIDS—which meant Ryan faced fear and prejudice, especially at school.

When his story captured the attention of the media, people felt bad for him; after all, he had not caught AIDS through sexual contact or intravenous drug use (he was a hemophiliac infected through a blood transfusion). Ryan, however, believed everyone living with the disease deserved compassion and support. He spoke out on behalf of all AIDS victims, appearing in magazines and on television shows. He also testified before the National Commission on AIDS. And he made friends with a superstar— Elton John.

When Ryan died in 1990, Elton was at his bedside. Later, Elton sang at the funeral. In his 2002 interview with Larry King, Elton said Ryan's death was a turning point in his life:

> **"I was probably at the height of my unhappiness. If you look back at footage of me [at the funeral], I looked like a 75-year-old white-haired . . . 300-pound man playing the piano. And I was really ashamed of myself."**

The Clean Life

Elton sought treatment for his many problems—drug addiction, alcoholism, and bulimia (an eating disorder). He told Larry King:

> **"It took me 16 years of drug addiction and alcoholism to actually have the humility to say, 'I need help.' . . . As soon as I said those words, . . . I was determined to get better. . . . And I've been sober now and clean for 11 years."**

Meanwhile, Elton's career was still moving forward. That year, "Sacrifice" was his first #1 hit in the UK—and it stayed #1 for six weeks. The following year, in 1991, a documentary, *Two Rooms*, described Elton's creative partnership with Bernie Taupin. Using the film as a springboard, a tribute album was also released, *Two Rooms: Celebrating the Songs of Elton John & Bernie Taupin*. Best of all, Elton's song "Basque" won a Grammy that year. Clearly, the clean life wasn't hurting Elton's career!

Who would've thought that a boy living in Indiana had the power to change the life of one of the world's biggest rock stars? But it's true. Ryan White (left) had AIDS, and all he wanted to do was live as normally as he could. Elton and Ryan became friends, and Ryan's courage inspired Elton to "get his act together."

The Meaning of Success

The 1990s turned out to be a good decade for Elton in many ways. Elton and Bernie signed a twelve-year $39 million deal with Warner/Chappell Music. Elton's 1992 album *The One* did well, and so did 1993's *Duets*, which was created in collaboration with fifteen other artists, including Tammy Wynette, RuPaul, Eric Clapton, and Kiki Dee.

A new opportunity came along for Elton in 1994: he was asked to write and perform the songs for Disney's *The Lion King*. The movie and the songs were hits that soon turned into classics, and Elton won another Grammy, this time for Best Male Pop Vocal Performance for "Can You Feel the Love Tonight." When the soundtrack was released, it remained

Elton worked with Tim Rice (right) in 1994 on the movie *The Lion King*, a Disney film. Elton's "Can You Feel the Love Tonight?" won him the Oscar for Best Original Song and Best Male Pop Vocal Performance. He dedicated the vocal award to his grandmother, who had made him play the piano.

at the top of *Billboard*'s charts for nine weeks; by 1999, it had sold 15 million copies, which meant it was considered a diamond record.

Elton's personal life was also going better. In 1993, he met the man who would become his permanent life partner, David Furnish, an advertising executive and filmmaker. Being sober and facing his problems meant that Elton could finally establish a stable personal relationship.

More honors came Elton's way in the 1990s. First, he and Bernie were **inducted** into the Songwriters' Hall of Fame, and then Elton made it into the Rock and Roll Hall of Fame. In recognition of his many achievements, his country gave him the even greater honor of becoming a Commander of the Order of the British Empire, and Queen Elizabeth made him a knight: Sir Elton John!

The 1990s were also the beginning of Elton's association with another rock pianist, Billy Joel. The two musicians were very different, and yet they had much in common. Billy Joel described his first meeting with Elton in an article in *Rolling Stone*:

> **"I told him what a fan I was, and he said he knew my stuff. I thought this was so cool: There were a thousand guitar players, but there were only two of us. The English piano player and the American piano player. . . . Elton gave a funny-looking guy like me—and so many others—an opportunity to be a singer-songwriter."**

When they toured together, they created a musical experience their fans loved.

Meanwhile, Elton kept writing new songs. His 1995 album, *Made in England*, and 1996's *Love Songs* were both favorably received. No wonder when Elton turned fifty in 1997, he celebrated in a big way! Dressed up in an $80,000 Louis XIV costume, he threw an enormous party for 500 of his friends.

The 1990s also had their difficult times. Elton lost two more close friends, Gianni Versace and Princess Diana. But Elton had learned the true meaning of success—and he knew it had as much to do with forming relationships and conquering his addictions as it did with fame and fortune.

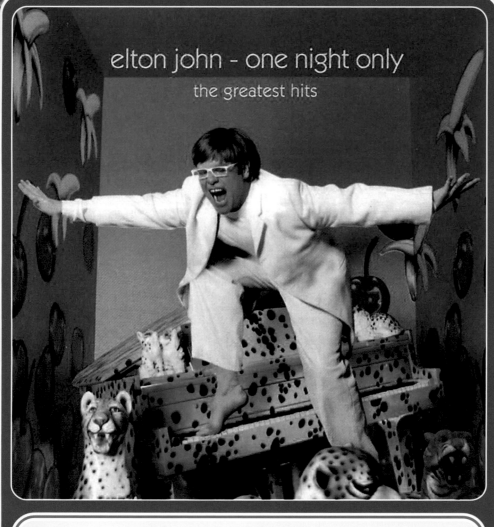

elton john - one night only
the greatest hits

As the new millennium approached, Elton was clean, happy, and still performing. In October 2000, Elton played a two-night concert series at New York City's Madison Square Garden. Though now a bit more subdued—at least in clothing and eyewear—he still put on a flamboyant performance that left the crowd cheering.

Elton the Legend

The new-and-improved Elton John was no saint. He still loved to spend his money on flamboyant clothes, lavish parties, and other luxuries. And he still wasn't afraid to speak out when he disagreed with someone, even to the point of going to court. And he wasn't afraid of offending people either.

Elton Speaks Out

Elton shocked quite a few people with his views on religion in an interview that was published in *The Observer*. He said:

> **"From my point of view I would ban religion completely, even though there are some wonderful things about it. I love the idea of the teachings of Jesus Christ and the beautiful stories about it, which I loved in Sunday school**

and I collected all the little stickers and put them in my book. But the reality is that organized religion doesn't seem to work. It turns people into hateful lemmings and it's not really compassionate. "

Elton was speaking as a gay person frustrated by the prejudice he saw practiced in the name of religion. Later, he pointed out that he was speaking of *organized* religion, rather than personal spirituality, but some people were still outraged.

But Elton hadn't become a legend by refusing to outrage people. In fact, his reputation has always been a mixture of honesty and flamboyance, kindness and nearly **decadent** generosity.

Collaborating with the Legend

Other artists' talents threaten some musicians. Elton, however, seems to be inspired by working with others. In the 2000s, he frequently collaborated with other musicians.

Tim Rice had worked with Elton on *The Lion King*, and in 2000, they worked together again to create songs for DreamWorks' animated movie, *The Road to El Dorado*; Elton was also the film's narrator. The two of them worked together again on the Disney production of *Aida*, for which they received the Tony Award for Best Original Score and a Grammy for Best Musical Show Album.

In October 2003, Elton announced that he was embarking on a different kind of collaboration: he and Celine Dion had signed an agreement to perform seventy-five shows over three years at Caesar's Palace on the Las Vegas Strip. Elton's show, *The Red Piano*, would be a multimedia concert featuring massive props and video montages created by David LaChapelle.

Elton also collaborated with other artists—including Alessandro Safina and British cellist Julian Lloyd Webber—to create several versions of "Your Song." Some of Elton's collaborations were more than just artistic endeavors; they were also acts of healing, as when he sang with Eminem at the Grammy Awards. By doing so, Elton helped clear Eminem of the accusations that he was prejudiced against homosexuals, and Elton paved the way for a greater mainstream acceptance of the rapper. Elton and Eminem's duet of "Stan" was included as a bonus track on Eminem's album *Curtain Call: The Hits*.

In October 2003, Elton and Celine Dion inked a unique deal with Caesar's Palace in Las Vegas, Nevada. Combined, the two agreed to perform seventy-five shows during a three-year period. *The Red Piano*, Elton's show, was more than a concert; it was a multimedia event, complete with huge props and elaborate video presentations!

When asked why he had chosen to pair up with someone who had a reputation for **homophobia**, Elton told VH1:

"I don't think he's homophobic. I wouldn't have done it if I thought he was, and he wouldn't have asked me to do it. We ended up hanging out for three days. He's a brilliant lyricist. If a person writes a novel and there's a homophobic scene in it, you don't say that the novelist is homophobic. I thought he had

a bad rap, and because I'm gay I came out and defended him. I'll defend his right to say what he wants to. I don't think he's hateful. 》

You might think Elton John and hip-hop would be an odd combination, but Elton is always open to new approaches to music. In September 2006, he told *Rolling Stone* magazine:

"I want to work with Pharrell, Timbaland, Snoop, Kanye, Eminem and just see what happens. It may be a disaster, it could be fantastic, but you don't know until you try. . . . I want to bring my songs and melodies to hip-hop beats. I love these beats, but I have no idea how to get them. 》

And Eminem wasn't the only rapper with whom Elton collaborated. Tupac's **posthumous** song "Ghetto Gospel" **sampled** Elton's 1971 song "Indian Sunset"; together, Tupac and Elton went all the way to #1 on the UK charts.

Elton made it to #1 with another collaboration as well, this time with the British boy-band Blue. Their version of "Sorry Seems to Be the Hardest Word" climbed the charts in many other European countries as well.

In May 2006, the limited edition of Pet Shop Boys' new album, *Fundamental*, included a new version of the 1989 song "In Private," recorded as a duet with Elton; it was later released as bonus track on Pet Shop Boys' top-20 hit "Minimal." Elton's string of UK #1 duets continued later that year when the Scissor Sisters released "I Don't Feel Like Dancin'," which Elton co-wrote. Recorded in Las Vegas, the song featured Elton on piano, and the Scissor Sisters included it on their album *Ta-Dah*. The song became the fourth-best-selling single in the UK in 2006 and it stayed in the UK top-40 lists for twenty-seven weeks. Elton also co-wrote "Intermission" from the same album.

As the decade drew to a close, Elton continued to team up with other musicians. In 2007, he was featured on the song "2 Man Show" in Timbaland's album *Timbaland Presents Shock Value*. Elton also made a guest appearance on Dr. Dre's 2007 album, *Detox*.

Can Elton Ever Retire from Songwriting?

In 2001, Elton had said that *Songs from the West Coast* would be his final studio album. He was getting older, after all, and he wanted to concentrate on his live performances.

He couldn't do it. Three years later, he released a new album, *Peachtree Road*. Elton just couldn't stop writing songs. His friend Billy Joel teased him about his productivity:

Rocket Man joins Piano Man. During the 1990s, Elton and Billy Joel teamed up for the Face-to-Face Tour. Elton performed some of Billy's best-known songs, and Billy sang and played some of Elton's hits. Then the dynamic duo performed a series of duets. Crowds all over the world were thrilled to see these two legends together.

" I haven't written a song since 1993, and he asks me, 'Billy, why don't you write some new songs?' I say, 'Elton, why don't you write less new songs?' At $200 a ticket, you can't shove new stuff down people's throats . . . : 'Rocket Man,' 'Crocodile Rock,' 'Bennie and the Jets,' 'Tiny Dancer,' and 'Your Song.' That's what they want to hear.**"**

Elton Goes to the Theater

Elton's work with Disney and DreamWorks had proved that his music combined well with a play or movie. His 1970s song "Tiny Dancer" was featured in the 2002 movie *Almost Famous*, and the following year, "The Heart of Every Girl" was the closing song for *Mona Lisa Smile*. In 2005, Elton returned to musical theater and composed music for playwright Lee Hall's *Billy Elliot the Musical*.

Elton had high hopes for a 2006 theatrical project with Bernie Taupin, *Lestat: The Musical*, based on the Anne Rice vampire novels. In his press release, he said:

"*Interview with the Vampire* is one of my favorite books and Anne Rice is one of my favorite authors. Although this project has taken a while to come together, I firmly believe we have the right team in place. *The Vampire Lestat* is the first stage musical that I've written with Bernie which makes it even more special for me.**"**

Bernie added:

"Anne had always loved the idea of seeing her Vampire Chronicles set in some sort of serious and seductive musical setting and for all of the parties involved this is the opportunity of a lifetime. Our intention is make a classically based show that is stripped of gothic clichés and that shows the vampire dealing with his damnation on a more realistic and human level. Please let me make this clear this is NOT a rock opera. Our hope is that it will be stylish, sexy, intelligent, rich and hypnotically dark."

Unfortunately, the play did not fare well. The critics panned it, and it closed after only thirty-nine performances.

The Legend Grows

Their musical may not have been a success, but an album they released the same year, *The Captain & the Kid*, was reviewed much more favorably. Like *Captain Fantastic and the Brown Dirt Cowboy*,

MALTA   Lm1.50

Valletta Bastions

eltonjohn
m a l t a   july 2003

The government of Malta released this set of Elton John postage stamps in 2003. Elton's music has been heard and appreciated by many people in many countries around the world for many years, and it doesn't look like that is going to change anytime soon.

the album was an autobiographical collection that reflected on Elton and Bernie's phenomenal forty-year partnership. It included ten new songs, including "The Bridge"—and the record cover, for the first time ever, showed Elton and Bernie together.

That same year, the Walt Disney Company named Elton a Disney Legend because of his many contributions to Disney films and theatrical works. This was a high honor—but Elton knew he was truly a legend when Madame Tussauds made a wax model of him. (It took more than a thousand hours to complete.)

Personal Celebrations

In December 2005, Elton and his partner David Furnish recognized their ongoing commitment to each other with a civil partnership, a legal ceremony in the UK that grants same-sex couples the same rights

December 2005 was a special time in Elton's personal life. He and David Furnish were joined in a civil partnership, which gives them the same rights as a married couple. In this photo, Elton and David are shown with Caroline Gruosi-Scheufele of Chopard, a watch company, at a benefit for one of Elton's many charities.

and responsibilities as those given by a civil marriage. The ceremony itself was simple and low-key, attended only by the couple's parents, two close friends, and their dog Arthur. Afterward, however, Elton and David threw one of Elton's typical lavish parties at their Berkshire mansion; it was rumored to have cost at least a million British pounds. The couple invited many famous individual to celebrate with them. Unfortunately, the guests were all delayed by the terrible traffic jam on the road leading to Elton's house!

Although Elton has never had any children of his own, kids are important to him. He especially enjoys his ten godchildren, including Sean Lennon, Elizabeth Hurley's son Damian, David and Victoria Beckham's son Brooklyn, and Seymour Stein's daughter. Would he ever consider children of his own? No, he told Y!Music.

> **"We've talked about adoption, but I think I'm too old. I don't want to be seventy years old and worrying about whether my daughter's doing crack."**

It's hard to connect the word "old" with Elton John, but in March 2007, he celebrated his sixtieth birthday. Who could believe the rock superstar was old enough to be a grandfather? In many ways, he seems as young as ever. At his party in Manhattan's Cathedral of St. John the Divine, more than three hundred of his friends joined him to wish him well. The star-studded party included actress Emma Thompson and actors Richard Gere and Michael Caine.

The following night, Elton marked the occasion of his sixtieth birthday with another landmark celebration: his sixtieth performance at New York City's Madison Square Garden. To celebrate the record he had set there for most performances, a banner proclaiming "Most Performances by a Single Artist" was raised to the rafters and then placed in the Madison Square Garden's Music Hall of Fame.

That night, Elton performed many of his classic songs, including all-time favorites like "Your Song," "Rocket Man," "Candle in the Wind," and "I'm Still Standing." Former president Bill Clinton introduced the birthday boy, and then actor Robin Williams led the audience in a chorus of "Happy Birthday." The show also featured behind-the-scenes footage from Elton's private party the night before, where his famous friends spoke of all they loved and admired about

Elton John has had, by anyone's definition, a phenomenal life and career. He's had lows, but Elton has always been able to bounce back from them stronger and better than ever. Though he's gotten older, suffered from some health issues, and might not be turning out the hits as often as he once did, Elton is still a musical force.

Elton. Meanwhile, the three-hour long and thirty-three–song concert streamed live via MSN Music. The concert was followed by a television special called *Happy Birthday Elton!* that aired on ITVI and MyNetwork TV.

A few days later, Elton celebrated his birthday yet again—and his years of musical achievement—with the release of a greatest-hits CD, *Rocket Man—Number Ones*. Also in March 2007, Elton's enormous musical legacy—nearly five hundred songs from thirty-two albums—

became available for legal download. In his statement to the media, he said:

> **I knew the entire catalog—not just the hits—needed care and attention to be released in this way. Now that it's happening, I'm pleased for the fans' sake.**

Who knows what lies ahead for the superstar? Considering all that he's achieved so far, there's really no way to tell. Elton told Y!Music:

> **I am a prolific kind of guy. It is quite amazing, I suppose; it's kind of wondrous how I squeezed it all in. I've tried lots of things; some of them have done well and some of them haven't, but at least I've tried them. . . . I suppose it is quite remarkable, but I'm more interested in 'What am I gonna do next?' I look forward.**

As Elton looks forward, one thing is certain: he's bound to keep making a difference in the world around him.

Elton John is an extraordinary musician. Even more important, he's an exceptional human being. Elton has given much of his time to a variety of humanitarian efforts, but his favorite charities involve the fight against AIDS. This photo was taken during a trip to South Africa to raise funds for AIDS victims in that country.

Making a Difference

Elton John had always been a generous person—but the Elton John who was reborn after Ryan White's death knew that it wasn't enough for him to make the occasional generous gesture. He needed to do more than that. He needed to work hard to make a difference in the world.

In a CNN interview, Elton said:

❝I've got to do something to make up for all those self-absorbed and selfish years when I just, you know, was taking drugs, sitting in my room, doing bad things, whatever.❞

The Fight Against AIDS

One of the big causes that is important to Elton, one where he feels called to do all he can to make a difference, is HIV/AIDS, the disease that has caused so many deaths in the gay community, the same disease that took the life of his good friend Ryan White.

After Ryan's death, Elton established the Elton John AIDS Foundation (EJAF), which would give 90 percent of its funds to direct care and 10 percent to AIDS prevention education. Elton also announced his intention to donate all future **royalties** from his singles to AIDS research.

Ryan's death wasn't the only time HIV/AIDS touched Elton's life. Elton had also been friends with Freddie Mercury, the rock group Queen's lead singer, who lost his life to AIDS two years after Ryan did. At a tribute concert for Freddie held at London's Wembley Stadium, Elton performed with the remaining members of Queen, singing the group's classic song "Bohemian Rhapsody," as well as "The Show Must Go On." "Bohemian Rhapsody" featured a duet with Elton and Axl Rose; this was yet another gesture of healing and reconciliation on Elton's part, since Rose had a reputation for being prejudiced against homosexuals. Proceeds from the concert benefited AIDS charities.

Even before Elton turned his life around, he did what he could for AIDS charities. In 1986, for example, he joined with Dionne Warwick, Gladys Knight, and Stevie Wonder to record "That's What Friends Are For"; all profits from the single were donated to the American Foundation for AIDS Research. (Later, the song also won Elton and the others a Grammy Award for Best Pop Performance by a Duo or Group with a Vocal.)

Today, EJAF continues to work for the prevention of HIV/AIDS, while it also fights prejudice and discrimination against HIV/AIDS-affected individuals and provides services to people living with or at risk of contracting HIV/AIDS. Elton is personally passionate about this cause, and in 2006, he donated a bright-red piano from his Las Vegas show to auction on eBay, with the proceeds going to raise funds for his foundation. He also hosts an annual White Tie and Tiara Ball, a glamorous event to which many celebrities are invited as a fund-raiser for Elton's foundation.

Ever since 2004, Elton has held a sale called "Elton's Closet," where he sells his own used clothing. Shopping for secondhand Elton John clothes, however, isn't anything like shopping at the Salvation Army, given the star's extravagant taste in clothes! In 2007, the 10,000 items sold in Elton's Closet raised more than $400,000 for AIDS/HIV research.

An online charity auction conducted through Tickets.com raised a half a million dollars for the Elton John AIDS Foundation. In this photo, W. Thomas Gimple of Tickets.com presents a check to Elton. The Elton John AIDS Foundation gives most of its funds to the direct care of people living with AIDS.

In November 2005, *Elton John's Christmas Party*, a compilation CD that included two Elton John Christmas songs as well as music by various other artists, was released exclusively at Starbucks coffee shops; two dollars from each sale was given to EJAF. The CD was re-released the following year for the 2006 Christmas season, once again as a fund-raiser for his foundation.

Live 8

On July 2, 2005, musicians got together for a series of concerts, held in various venues around the world. These concerts, called Live 8, were timed to precede the G8 Conference, where the eight most powerful countries would discuss the world's economy. Live 8 sought to pressure the world's leaders to drop the debt owed by the world's poorest nations, while they increased the aid they gave to these same poverty-stricken countries.

Elton was one of several performers who participated in Live 8 on July 2, 2005. The goal was to raise awareness of the plight of the world's poorest nations. Listeners were urged to contact their G8 representatives and ask them to reduce poor countries' debt loads. That way, they could help themselves in fighting hunger and the effects of AIDS.

Elton John was one of the performers at the Live 8 concert held in London's Hyde Park. As he sang "The Bitch Is Back," "Saturday Night's Alright for Fighting," and "Children of the Revolution" (this one with the Libertines and Pete Doherty), he was raising his voice on behalf of those who were too poor to have a voice of their own. On July 7, the G8 leaders pledged to double the 2004 levels of aid to Africa from US$25 billion to US$50 billion by the year 2010. Elton and the other musicians, however, knew there was still much more work to be done.

A Changed Man

As Elton looks back on his life, some of his past behaviors make him cringe.

> **"I could be unbelievably horrid and stupid. On tours I'd get on a plane, then get off it, maybe six or eight times. I'd walk out of a hotel suite because I didn't like the color of the bedspread. I remember looking out of my room at the Inn on the Park one day and saying, 'It's too windy. Can someone please do something about it?'"**

He's come a long way since those spoiled superstar days. Nowadays, Elton knows what his priorities are. On EJAF's Web site, a letter from Elton states:

> **"The most meaningful part of my public life is my work as a humanitarian in the global effort to end the AIDS epidemic. . . . When our lives are done, won't we want it to be said that when we saw millions of people suffering, millions more at risk, millions more abandoned, a whole continent in danger of dying— we stood up and REFUSED to let it happen?"**

1949 Reginald Dwight (Elton John) is born.

1964 Reginald formed a band called Bluesology with friends.

1965 Bluesology performs as a backup band for American artists.

1966 Bluesology becomes the supporting band for Long John Baldry.

1967 Reginald Dwight changes his name to Elton John.

The first collaboration between Bernie Taupin and Elton is released.

1968 Elton and Bernie sign a songwriting contract with DJM Records.

1969 Elton's debut album *Empty Sky* is released in the U.K.

1970 *Elton John* is released in both the U.K. and the U.S.

1972 *Honky Château* becomes Elton's first #1 album in the United States.

1974 Elton collaborates with former Beatle John Lennon.

1975 Elton plays the Pinball Wizard in the rock opera *Tommy* by The Who.

1977 Elton announces he's retiring from concert performances.

1980 **September** Elton performs at a free concert in New York's Central Park.

1984 Elton marries Renate Blauel; they divorce four years later.

1985 Elton performs at Live Aid.

1986 A history of heavy marijuana use contributes to Elton's loss of his voice.

Elton receives his first Grammy.

1988 Elton performs at five sold-out shows at Madison Square Garden.

1990 Elton performs at the funeral of Ryan White.

Elton enters rehab to combat a history of drug abuse, alcoholism, and eating disorders.

1991 A documentary on Elton's and Bernie's creative process is released.

1992 Bernie and Elton are inducted into the Songwriters Hall of Fame.

Elton establishes the Elton John AIDS Foundation.

1994 Disney asks Elton to write and perform songs for *The Lion King*.

Elton is inducted into the Rock and Roll Hall of Fame.

1995 Elton is made a Commander of the Order of the British Empire.

1996 Disney names Elton a Disney Legend, its highest honor.

1997 **September 6** Elton performs a new version of "Candle in the Wind" at the funeral of Princess Diana.

1998 Queen Elizabeth knights Elton in recognition of his charity work.

1999 Elton and Tim Rice work together on *Aida*, which brings the pair a Tony Award and Grammy.

2000 Elton creates songs and is narrator for the film *The Road to El Dorado*.

2002 "Tiny Dancer" is featured in *Almost Famous*.

2003 Elton and Celine Dion sign a seventy-five show deal with Caesar's Palace.

"The Heart of Every Girl" is the closing song for *Mona Lisa Smiles*.

2004 Elton receives a Kennedy Center Honor.

2005 Elton composes the music for the theater's *Billy Elliot the Musical*.

July 2 Elton performs at Live 8.

December 21 Elton enters a civil partnership with David Furnish.

2006 The Bernie/Elton collaboration *Lestat: The Musical* opens on Broadway, closing after thirty-nine performances.

2007 **March** Elton performs his sixtieth concert at Madison Square Garden.

Elton's music catalog becomes available for legal download.

Selected Albums

1969 *Empty Sky* (released in the U.S. in 1975)
1970 *Elton John*
1971 *11-17-70*; *Madman Across the Water*; *Tumbleweed Connection*
1972 *Honky Château*
1973 *Don't Shoot Me I'm Only the Piano Player*; *Goodbye Yellow Brick Road*
1974 *Caribou*
1975 *Captain Fantastic and the Brown Dirt Cowboy*; *Rock of the Westies*
1976 *Blue Moves*; *Here and There*
1978 *A Single Man*
1979 *Victim of Love*
1980 *21 at 33*
1981 *The Fox*
1982 *Jump Up!*
1983 *Too Low for Zero*
1984 *Breaking Hearts*
1985 *Ice on Fire*
1986 *Leather Jackets*
1987 *Live in Australia with the Melbourne Symphony Orchestra*
1988 *Reg Strikes Back*
1989 *Sleeping with the Past*
1992 *The One*
1993 *Duets*
1995 *Made in England*
1997 *The Big Picture*
2000 *One Night Only*
2001 *Songs from the West Coast*
2002 *Live at the Ritz*
2004 *Peachtree Road*
2006 *The Captain & the Kid*

Number-One Singles

1970 "Your Song"
1972 "Rocket Man"
         "Crocodile Rock"
1973 "Goodbye Yellow Brick Road"
1974 "Bennie and the Jets"
         "Don't Let the Sun Go Down on Me"
         "Lucy in the Sky with Diamonds"

1975 "Philadelphia Freedom"
"Island Girl"
1976 "Don't Go Breaking My Heart" (with Kiki Dee)
1983 "I Guess That's Why They Call It the Blues"
1987 "Candle in the Wind"
1989 "Through the Storm" (with Aretha Franklin)
1991 "Don't Let the Sun Go Down on Me" (with George Michael)
1997 "Something About the Way You Look Tonight"
"Candle in the Wind '97"

Videos
2000 *The Very Best of Elton John*
2001 *One Night Only: The Greatest Hits Live at Madison Square Garden*
2002 *Live in Barcelona*
2004 *Dream Ticket*
To Russia with Elton
2007 *Music in Review—Elton John*

Awards and Recognitions
1986 Grammy Award: Best Pop Performance by a Duo or Group with Vocal ("That's What Friends Are For").

1991 Grammy Award: Best Instrumental Composition ("Basque").

1992 Elton and Bernie Taupin are inducted into the Songwriters Hall of Fame.

1994 Grammy Award: Best Male Pop Vocal Performance ("Can You Feel the Love Tonight?"); Elton is inducted into Rock and Roll Hall of Fame.

1995 Queen Elizabeth II names Elton a Commander of the Order of the British Empire.

1996 Disney names Elton a Disney Legend.

1997 Grammy Award: Best Male Pop Vocal Performance ("Candle in the Wind 1997").

1998 Queen Elizabeth II knights Elton in recognition of his charitable work.

2000 Grammy Award: Best Musical Show Album (*Elton John & Tim Rice's Aida*); Tony Award: Original Musical Score (*Aida*, with Tim Rice).

2004 Receives a Kennedy Center Honor.

Books

Cassata, Mary Anne, and Jim Turano. *The Elton John Scrapbook.* New York: Citadel, 2002.

Flynn, Paul. *Dream Ticket: Elton John Across Four Decades.* New York: HST Management, 2004.

Jackson, Jane (ed.). *Chorus of Light: Photographs from the Sir Elton John Collection.* New York: Rizzoli, 2001.

Norman, Philip. *Sir Elton: The Definitive Biography.* New York: Carroll & Graff, 2001.

O'Mahoney, John. *World Musicmakers—Elton John.* Farmington Hills, Mich.: Blackbirch Press, 2003.

Rosenthal, Elizabeth. *His Song: The Musical Journey of Elton John.* New York: Billboard Books, 2001.

White, Katherine. *Elton John.* New York: Rosen, 2002.

Web Sites

www.ejaf.org
Elton John AIDS Foundation

www.eltonography.com
The Illustrated Elton John Discography

www.eltonjohn.com
Elton John Official Web Site

www.gusdudgeonfoundation.com
The Gus Dudgeon Foundation for Recording Arts

www.rockhall.com
Rock and Roll Hall of Fame

big band—A large jazz or dance band, especially popular in the 1930s and 1940s.

boogie-woogie—A jazz piano style derived from the blues.

covered—Recorded something previously released and made well known by another artist.

decadent—Showing uninhibitedly self-indulgent behavior.

denigrate—To defame or criticize somebody or something.

flamboyant—Showy, brightly colored, and elaborate in a self-satisfied way.

gospel—Highly emotional religious music that originated among African American Christians in the southern United States.

homophobia—An irrational hatred, disapproval, or fear of homosexuality and homosexuals.

inducted—Formally admitted into an organization.

memorabilia—Objects associated with a famous person or event.

posthumous—Occurring after someone's death.

prolific—Highly productive.

R&B—Rhythm and blues; a style of music originally developed by African American musicians and that combines elements of blues and jazz.

royalties—Percentages of income from a book, piece of music, or invention that are paid to its creator.

sampled—Used a piece music taken from an existing recording as part of a new recording.

soul—A style of African American music with a strong emotional quality, related to gospel music and rhythm and blues.

stoic—Appearing to be unaffected by emotions.

venue—Location for an event or concert.

Ethan Schlesinger lives in upstate New York, where he is a freelance author.

Picture Credits

page

  2: Newswire Photo Service
  8: Anwar Hussein/WENN
11: Giuseppe Farinacci/AFP
12: KRT/PressLink
14: Rocket Record Co./UPI
17: Pictorial Press
19: Pictorial Press
20: New Millennium Images
23: Rex Features
25: Rex Features
26: National Film Archive
29: BBC/Star Photos
30: New Millennium Images

32: Sardine Photos
35: HHHS/KRT
36: UPI Photo Archive
38: Universal Records/NMI
41: Newswire Photo Service
43: Bill Greenblatt/UPI Photo
45: Newswire Photo Service
46: Chopard/PRNPS
48: UPI Newspictures
50: Feature Photo Service
53: Feature Photo Service
54: kguk-42/INFGoff

Front cover: Newswire Photo Service